A Reflective Journal for Busy People

100 Affirmations of Health, Happiness, Prosperity, and Wisdom

By
Gale Lyman,
RN, BSN, HN-BC

Note to the reader: This book is intended as an informational guide. The approach and technique described herein are meant to supplement, and not to be substituted for professional medical care or treatment.

ISBN: 978-0-615-34286-3

To order directly from the publisher order on line at www.lulu.com.

Author inquires can be directed to Gale Lyman at info@lymancenter.com.

Designed with Garamond font to use less ink, and printed on demand to minimize the impact on our beautiful forests.

Photography by Gale Lyman.

Acknowledgements with gratitude....

I am grateful for the experiences that guided me to create these affirmations.

I am grateful to my teachers, colleagues, and favorite authors for wisdom and inspiration. Sue and Aaron Singleton, Janet Desaulnier, Sarah Ban Breathnach, Veda Andrus, Marie Shanahan, Sharon Clark, Hawaya Takata, Kay Bise, Ilan Shamir, Amy Bachelor, Raylene Cashman Parker, Sandy Sudol, Alyssa Whitefeather Nock, Barbara Brennan, Barbara James, Belleruth Naparstek, Marcia Goodwin Blair, Deanna Smith, Marianne Quirk, Janice Anderson, Louise Hay, Cie Simurro, Kathy Carey, Nanette Masi, Kelly Nickerson and Linda Williams.

I am grateful to my husband and my family.

I am grateful to my assistants, proof readers, editors, and publishers.

I am grateful to you, dear reader, for allowing me to share the practice of self reflection and affirmation with you.

Thank you,

Gale

Preface

Many of us desire better health, more happiness, added prosperity, and insightful wisdom, but these yearnings remain unfulfilled. How can you be what you want to be? What do you do? What do you change?

This journal provides inspiration for health, happiness, prosperity, and wisdom. With it, you can create a place, a time, and a means for self reflection.

Use self reflective journaling to access the healing and insight within you. There you will find the answers you seek. Then use the affirmations provided to manifest what you desire.

You can achieve your goals for health, happiness, prosperity, and wisdom. Be present, trust, and listen to your heart. Be at peace.

In gratitude for being part of your life,

Gale

The Basic User's Guide

If you want something that you don't have, something needs to change. Self reflection helps you to discover what and how to change. Then affirmations become the catalyst for change. It is that simple, and that profound.

- ♥ Accept the need for change.
- ♥ Practice self reflection to determine what and how to change.
- ♥ Use affirmations to launch the new thoughts, attitudes, behaviors, and action that will lead to what your heart desires.

This is the simple recipe for health, happiness, prosperity and wisdom.

The Read and Go User's Guide (for exceptionally busy people)

- ♥ Read an affirmation and repeat it to yourself several times during the day.

The Concise User's Guide

- ♥ Read the affirmation
- ♥ Write or sketch anything you want in response. If you are stuck, try these questions:
    - ♥ What does the affirmation mean to you?
    - ♥ Do you agree?
    - ♥ Is this a goal for you?
    - ♥ Are there other words that better express this affirmation for you?

More wonderful ideas from our readers

- ♥ Keep the journal by your bedside or in your purse
- ♥ Follow the affirmations sequentially.
- ♥ Or, randomly open the book to any page, trusting the ideal affirmation for that day will be there.
- ♥ Work with one affirmation a day, or perhaps one a week, or even one a month
- ♥ If the page seems too big or too blank, draw lines to divide it into quarters.
- ♥ When you finish, begin again, noting growth or a greater willingness to explore.

For a more comprehensive user's guide, read on...

An Introduction to Affirmations, Self reflection, and Journaling

Affirmations

Affirmations accept self responsibility for creating what you desire. Perceptions, attitudes, and beliefs become reality. Thoughts and action manifest desires. Love and gratitude connect us with each other and to Something Greater (whatever that may be in your personal beliefs or religion.)

Becoming something different, perhaps at peace instead of stressed, or financially balanced instead of in debt, requires change. That doesn't always mean that we have to do more, or move, or change jobs. Often, being different is more important than doing differently. Be open to change.

Release your expectations. Consider the affirmation, "I am supported in my efforts to care for myself." If you think the answer to this affirmation is for your spouse or your boss to become more supportive, you may ignore the friend or colleague who is trying to support you. Or you may miss the new human resource policy that supports your intention, or the synchronicity of meeting the ideal helper at the ideal time.

Immediate change happens, at least within you, when you state your affirmation during tough times. Change is difficult when your environment, including the people in your life, challenge what you affirm. Your own negative thoughts may even oppose you. "I am financially balanced" is a tough affirmation to maintain, when a large unexpected bill arrives or your thoughts are centered on not earning enough money. Rather than give up, continue to focus your thoughts and ultimately your actions on being financially balanced.

Lasting change happens incrementally when you repeat affirmations several times a day.

Effective affirmations are full sentences, written in the present tense. "I eat healthy foods" instead of "I will eat healthy foods."

Compelling affirmations are positive; "I breath fresh air" as opposed to "I don't smoke."

Successful affirmations focus on what you want. The Law of Attraction says you receive that on which you focus. "I release all fear and fill its place with love" puts fear first. "I am filled with love" is stronger, emphasizing the love you desire.

Sometimes an affirmation seems too difficult for long term commitment. In those instances, adding "Just for today..." as an antecedent may help your affirmation seem more feasible. It is a way of walking before you run. But be sure to reaffirm every day, and when you are ready to run, drop the "just for today" phrase.

Authentic affirmations use words that have conscious meaning for you. For example, "I am happy" is most effective when you have defined happiness. I define happiness as loving and being loved, and being delighted by all around me. When I affirm "I am happy" this is what I mean.

In the beginning and at the end of this journal, you will find an opportunity to pause and reconsider, "What do health, happiness, prosperity, and wisdom mean to you?" Most people are surprised to find that their opinions change.

Repeat your favorite affirmations often. With the borders located in the back of the journal, create a reminder for yourself by framing and displaying an affirmation.

Self Reflection

Time for reflection is missing from our busy lifestyle. Unless created with great determination, the opportunity to think about what you mean to do, or about what has happened, is absent. Life just happens, often occurring *to* you rather than *with* you.

And yet, reflection leads to things that we do value. Focus, creativity, presence, self-awareness, wisdom, solutions, awareness of consequences, and recognition of possibilities.

With self reflection, you can find out what you want, what is keeping you from your desires, and what to do about it.

This journal offers you one affirmation per page, with plenty of available space. Use the space for self reflective journaling or sketching, continuing on the blank pages at the end of the journal if needed. Spend some time in self reflection. Write from your heart. Then express your thoughts and argue, ignore, adopt, or co-create the affirmation.

If you like, you may begin self reflection with these words.

Comfort and support my body-mind-spirit
during this period of growth and change.
Support my intention to release old outdated beliefs
and to embrace the new.
Raise me to the highest potential of self-care,
the highest level of health, happiness, prosperity, and
wisdom.
Clear out all unnecessary baggage
and lead me to my authentic self, my life purpose.

Conscious Breathing

Conscious breathing can enhance your practice of self reflection. It will still your thoughts, and allow you to go deeper into your consciousness. Focusing on your breath can bypass your busy mind and your preset responses to arrive at the heart of a matter.

Try breathing in deeply, and as you breathe out completely, state an affirmation out loud or in your heart. Repeat this several times. Notice any thoughts that interfere. Gently release thoughts that are distracting. When you are done meditating, write or sketch the insights that were helpful.

Prayer

The role of prayer in your affirmation and reflection practice will depend upon your personal beliefs.

Prayer is integral to everything in my life. I pray petitions for what I am affirming. I pray for help and support as I grow and change. I pray with gratitude. I pray with thanksgiving.

Most affirmations are easily modified to be prayers. For example, "My heart and soul are filled with joy" becomes "Dear Lord, Fill my heart and soul with joy" or "Thank you, God, for the joy that fills my heart and soul."

Journaling Examples

"I am grateful for blue sky and sunshine."

My mind is calm, like a blue sky on a warm, sunny day.

All thoughts I no longer need float away like puffy, white clouds.

"I am at peace."

What does this mean to me? At first, I think of "peace on earth", like a white dove. That feels out of my reach, beyond my ability. Yet, I value peace. As I repeat it, my focus is shifted to me being at peace. Mind your own business, my mom always said!

And yet, minding my own business, minding my own peacefulness, must contribute in some way to global peace. Even this objective, being at peace, seems difficult yet more achievable than affecting peace on the planet. I am not always at peace, but I would like to be.

Conclusion

Remember the simple recipe for health, happiness, prosperity and wisdom.

- ♥ Accept the need for change.
- ♥ Practice self reflection to determine what and how to change.
- ♥ Use affirmations to launch the new thoughts, attitudes, behaviors, and action that will lead to what your heart desires.

Love and care for yourself always, and especially during this time of growth. May you find all that you desire, and more.

100 Affirmations of Health, Happiness, Prosperity, and Wisdom

What do health, happiness, prosperity, and wisdom mean to you?

True health

      Affirmation: *I am healthy.*

      Describe or sketch health.

Authentic happiness

      Affirmation: *I am happy.*

      Describe or sketch happiness.

_____

Genuine prosperity

Affirmation: *I am prosperous.*

Describe or sketch prosperity.

Real wisdom

Affirmation: *I am wise.*

Describe or sketch wisdom.

I accept gradual change, incremental change.

_____

My body-mind-spirit-emotions are harmonious as I grow and change into my authentic self.

I am supported in my efforts to care for myself.

_____

I have the courage and the strength that I need to change.

There is an abundance of light, love, and money in my life, for all the things I want and need.

―――――――――――――――――――

I release the root cause of my pain.

I am awake. Relaxed, but awake.

_____

I am balanced in body, mind, spirit, & emotions.

I lead from a place of balance.

Just for today, I care for my physical body.

_____

I am filled with strength, wisdom, and grace.

_____

Just for today, I believe in myself.

I have the courage to fulfill my life's purpose.

———————————————————————————

Just for today, my physical body is in ideal alignment.

_____

Just for today, I am awake, aware, and at rest.

_____

I am conscious of the possibilities around me.

I am conscious of the beauty and
knowledge that surround me.

———————————————————

I release my physical pain and any
attachment to it.

I am grateful that I am surrounded by love.

———————————————————————————

I am grateful to be a member of my family.

_____

I am grateful for blue sky and sunshine.

_____

I am grateful for the comfort in my life.

_____

I earn a healthy salary.

_____

I stand straight with dignity, but bend with the breeze.

———————————————

I enjoy healthy, nourishing foods.

_____

I live simply.

I am beautiful.

I am flexible.

I visualize what I want to be.

_____

I manifest goodness and love.

_____

I ask for help.

Cash flows freely in and out, ideally balanced.

I love and am loved.

_____

I use resources appropriately.

I take care of myself.

I act and speak my truth from a place of love.

_____

I accept gifts and blessings.

_____

I patiently persevere.

Abundant loving energy fills me and flows through me.

_____

I listen.

I understand.

Vitality fills me.

———————————————————————————

I am open to accept healing.

_____

My energy flows freely.

I am filled with only light and love.

Everything I need and want is here for me.

_____

I am open to future possibilities.

———————————————————————————————

I am.

I am centered.

I express my emotions then release them.

I laugh.

I am organized.

I release structure.

———————————————————————————

I am present.

I continuously work on my own healing, fully conscious of how that affects others and the environment.

———————————————————

I have a continuous supply of the ideal amount of money, attained with grace and ease.

I feel good.

I am able to do what I want to do.

I am a healing presence to all in my environment.

_____

I am balanced within and in harmony
without.

My heart is open.

_____

I am filled with peace.

I eat foods that make me feel healthy.

I move in fun ways that make me feel
good.

I attract and expect ideal opportunities to maximize my health.

———————————————————————

I discern what will maximize my health.

I attract expert advice and wisdom.

_____

I hold onto my dream.

I release expectations, like financial and other "achievement" milestones, knowing that what I achieve may be greater than my wildest dreams.

I do my best and let go of how my work is received by friends, family colleagues, clients, students, publishers, the world…!

I sleep well.

My immune system is strong and resilient.

_____

I am at peace.

I am full of vitality.

My home and gardens are full of love and things of beauty.

_____

I walk for the joy of it, surrounded by nature.

I am balanced as I move forward with change.

_____

The energy in my home is pure.

The abundance of the universe flows
freely to me for my greater good.

_____

The abundance of the universe flows freely through me for the greater good of all.

I say yes when offered support.

I believe my inner wisdom.

I trust my intuition.

I effectively use my knowledge and my abilities.

_____

I balance, with grace, ease, and gratitude, everything that I want in my life.

I am financially serene.

I am financially balanced.

_____

I am financially abundant and grateful.

_____

I lead my team in a way that it achieves its mission infinitely.

_____

I have a continuous supply of the ideal amount of money for our household's work, our wants, and our needs.

———————————————————————

I co create my work in a way so that it continuously attracts ideal clients, employees, and expert helpers at the ideal time.

My work creates an income that meets
our household wants and needs with
abundance.

I am balanced and clear of any energy patterns interfering in what I want, who I am, and what I do.

_____

My heart is filled with Love.

I send Peace out into the world.

My energy patterns support what I want, who I am, and what I do.

_____

I go with the flow, like a hawk soaring
with the breeze.

_____

Today and every day, I have all the time I need.

I am happy, healthy, prosperous, and wise.

_____

What do health, happiness, prosperity, and wisdom mean to you?

True health

> Affirmation: *I am healthy.*
>
> Describe or sketch health.

Authentic happiness

> Affirmation: *I am happy.*
>
> Describe or sketch happiness.

_____

Genuine prosperity

    Affirmation: *I am prosperous.*

    Describe or sketch prosperity.

Real wisdom

    Affirmation: *I am wise.*

    Describe or sketch wisdom.

As you go forward…

Hold onto your dream, your life's purpose.

Let go of your expectations.

Accept the growth, healing, and change required to receive your desires.

And may your affirmations be realized at their highest potential.

Frame and display an affirmation

✄

Notes and sketches

_____

Notes and sketches

Notes and sketches

_____

Notes and sketches

Notes and sketches

Gale Lyman, RN, BSN, CCM, HN-BC, is a board certified holistic nurse and the founder of The Lyman Center in Amesbury, Massachusetts. Gale's life-long work is to help people take better care of themselves and to promote the integration of the holistic paradigm with conventional healthcare.

Gale is available for workshops, retreats, and private healing sessions. She is skilled in many holistic modalities that facilitate well-being and healing, including guided imagery, Reiki, sound healing, breathwork, meditation, journaling, affirmations, and all manner of relaxation exercises.

For more information, visit www.LymanCenter.com

www.ingramcontent.com/pod-product-compliance
Lightning Source LLC
LaVergne TN
LVHW091154080426

835509LV00006B/681